SCIENTIFIC AMERICAN. EDUCATIONAL PUBLISHING

T0046641

HUMAN BIOLOGY

10 FUN

EXPERIMENTS INVESTIGATING THE BODY

BRING SCIENCE HOME

Published in 2024 by Scientific American Educational Publishing in association with
The Rosen Publishing Group 29 East 21st Street, New York, NY 10010

Contains material from Scientific American , a division of Springer Nature America, Inc., reprinted by permission as well as original material from The Rosen Publishing Group .

Editor: Emily Mahoney
Designer: Rachel Rising

Activity on page 5 by Science Buddies/Svenja Lohner (November 28, 2019); Activity on page 9 by Science Buddies/Sabine De Brabandere (August 9, 2018); Activity on page 15 by Science Buddies/Sabine De Brabandere (March 22, 2018); Activity on page 19 by Science Buddies/Svenja Lohner (November 10, 2016); Activity on page 25 by Science Buddies (May 30, 2013); Activity on page 31 by Science Buddies (January 2, 2014); Activity on page 37 by Science Buddies (November 14, 2013); Activity on page 43 by Science Buddies (February 7, 2013); Article on page 47 by Science Buddies (March 31, 2016); Article on page 53 by Science Buddies (August 31, 2012).

All illustrations by Continuum Content Solutions

Photo Credits: pp. 3, 4, 5 , 8, 12, 13, 17, 18, 19, 22, 23, 25, 28, 29, 34, 35, 40, 43, 45, 46, 47, 51, 52, 56, 57 cve iv/ Shutterstock.com; pp. 4, 5, 9, 15, 19, 25, 31, 37, 43, 47, 53 Anna Frajtova/Shutterstock.com.

Library of Congress Cataloging-in-Publication Data

Names: Scientific American, inc., editor. | Scientific American Educational
    Publishing.
Title: Human biology : 10 fun experiments investigating the body /
    Scientific American Editors.
Other titles: 10 fun experiments investigating the body
Description: Buffalo, New York : Scientific American Educational
    Publishing, an imprint of Rosen Publishing, [2024] | Series: Bring
    science home | Includes index. | Audience: Grades 7-9
Identifiers: LCCN 2022059974 (print) | LCCN 2022059975 (ebook) | ISBN
    9781725349131 (library binding) | ISBN 9781725349124 (paperback) | ISBN
    9781725349148 (ebook)
Subjects: LCSH: Human biology--Experiments--Juvenile literature. | Human
    physiology--Experiments--Juvenile literature. | Human
    body--Experiments--Juvenile literature. | Science projects--Juvenile
    literature. | Biology projects--Juvenile literature.
Classification: LCC QP37 .H86 2024 (print) | LCC QP37 (ebook) | DDC
    612.0078--dc23/eng/20230127
LC record available at https://lccn.loc.gov/2022059974
LC ebook record available at https://lccn.loc.gov/2022059975

Manufactured in the United States of America

Some of the images in this book illustrate individuals who are models. The depictions do not imply actual situations or events.

CPSIA Compliance Information: Batch #SACS24. For further information contact Rosen Publishing, New York, New York at 1-800-237-9932.

Find us on

CONTENTS

⚛ THESE ACTIVITIES INCLUDE
   SCIENCE FAIR PROJECT IDEAS.

INTRODUCTION

The human body is amazing. There are many systems working together to make your body function every day. But how much do you really know about how your body works? The fun and interesting experiments in this book will help you to discover more about how your human body is able to do fascinating things!

Projects marked with ⚛ include a section called Science Fair Project Ideas. These ideas can help you develop your own original science fair project. Science fair judges tend to reward creative thought and imagination, and it helps if you are really interested in your project. You will also need to follow the scientific method. See page 61 for more information about that.

Test the Strength of Hair

DISCOVER THE SURPRISING STRENGTH OF A RENEWABLE BIOLOGICAL MATERIAL: HAIR!

Have you ever wondered how strong hair is? When we talk about our hair, we usually discuss color, length, or texture. But what about hair strength? If you look at a strand of hair, it looks like a very thin string. In fact, it is on average only about 0.004 inch (0.1 mm) thick. It doesn't seem like such a thin string could be very strong. How much weight do you think a single strand of hair can carry? In this activity, you will put a piece of hair to the test and find out. You might be surprised by your results!

PROJECT TIME
15 minutes

KEY CONCEPTS
Biology
Physiology
Physics
Mechanical strength

5

BACKGROUND

Did you know that an average person's head has about 100,000 hairs? Each one of these hairs grows out of a hair follicle, which is a tunnel-shaped structure in the outer layer of our skin. You might have noticed that at its root a hair sometimes has a whiter and softer texture than the rest of the hair. This part of the hair, which is usually beneath the skin, is called the hair bulb. It is the living portion of the hair and is responsible for hair growth. The other part of the hair, which we see growing out of our skin, is called the hair shaft.

The hair shaft is primarily responsible for our hair's strength. You might be surprised to hear that although a hair shaft is on average only 0.004 inch (0.1 mm) thick, it is made up of three different layers. The innermost layer at the hair's center is called the medulla. It is almost invisible and very soft and fragile. The middle layer is the thickest layer and is called the cortex. Much of its strength comes from a material called keratin. Keratin is also found in our fingernails, as well as animals' feathers, hoofs, and claws. In this layer, the keratin is arranged in rodlike bundles—alongside fats that add additional structure. The cortex also houses the melanin pigments that give our hair its color. The outermost layer of the hair shaft is called the cuticle. This layer is formed by flat, overlapping layers of cells that form scales, similar to fish scales, which strengthen and protect the hair shaft. Together these three layers create a very strong hair fiber.

In this activity, you will test how strong one single hair strand is by measuring how much weight it can carry. You don't even have to pull any hair—you can simply use one of the approximately 100 hairs that a person loses on average each day!

MATERIALS

At least one hair strand (at least 2 inches [5 cm] long). This can be collected from a brush or comb or elsewhere.
Pencil
Two stacks of books or two same-sized boxes
Paper clip
Tape
Small plastic bag
Small items to use as weights (such as pennies, marbles, and so forth)
Scale
Additional strands of hair, including some from different people (optional)

PREPARATION

- Tie one end of a hair strand securely around the middle of the pencil. If making a knot is too difficult, you can tape the hair to the pencil.

- Attach the other end of the hair strand to a paperclip (using a knot or tape).

- Hook the paperclip through the top of one side of the small plastic bag.

- Test whether the hair holds on to the pencil and bag by pulling on both ends slightly. If the hair comes loose, use more tape to secure the hair.

- Stack two piles of books or boxes to the same height—tall enough to accommodate the length of the hair and plastic bag. Place the stacks next to each other, leaving a gap between them that is wide enough so that the pencil balances across the stacks and the bag hangs freely in the gap.

PROCEDURE

- Before you start your test, guess how much weight the hair will be able to carry. *How many pennies or marbles do you think it will take to break the hair?*

- Take one of your weights (pennies or marbles) and carefully place it into the plastic bag. *Does the hair break?*

- If the hair is still intact, gently add another penny or marble to the bag. *What happens to the hair when you add this additional weight?*

- Continue to add weight to the bag. Inspect the hair carefully after adding each weight. *How does the hair hold up with increasing weight?*

Once the hair breaks, place the plastic bag, including the pennies or marbles that are inside, on the scale. *How much weight was the hair able to carry? Was it more or less than you predicted in the beginning?*

ExTRA

Repeat the same test with hair from different people. *Which hair was the strongest?*

ExTRA

Instead of using one strand of hair, try the test with two or more strands of hair tied in parallel. *Can two strands of hair carry double the weight?*

⚛ SCIENCE FAIR IDEA

Find out if hair texture makes a difference. *Does curly hair or straight hair carry more weight?*

OBSERVATIONS AND RESULTS ··········

How much weight was your strand of hair able to carry? Did your results surprise you? Although a single strand of hair looks very thin and fragile, it can carry a weight of up to 3.5 ounces (100 g). This is because of the three-layered structure of the hair shaft and also the strong keratin fibers that make up the middle layer, or the cortex, of the hair strand. How many grams would you estimate all of a person's hair could hold?

CLEANUP ··········

Put all materials away where you found them and throw the hair(s) in the garbage.

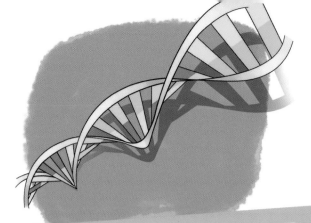

Colorful Double Helix

HOW DOES YOUR DNA COPY ITSELF SO PRECISELY?
TRY THIS MATCHING PAIRS ACTIVITY AND FIND OUT!

PROJECT TIME

30 minutes

KEY CONCEPTS

Biology
Life
DNA
Double helix

Ever wondered how DNA, the genetic blueprint of a life-form, can encode and pass on the information on how to grow and maintain that life-form? Just like a cookbook contains a recipe for a dish, DNA stores the recipe for the life of an organism. Unlike various recipes, however, very different organisms' DNA, such as in a fungus, plant, or animal, all look very similar. Although each human has a unique DNA sequence, the DNA in all of us is about 99.9 percent identical! In this activity you will make a model for a short section of DNA—enough to get a sense of what it is like and how it encodes life.

9

BACKGROUND

Plants, fungi, and animals might seem very different from one another, but they are all made up of tiny building blocks called cells, and—with very few exceptions—each of these cells has in its center a molecule containing the organism's blueprint. This molecule is called DNA: deoxyribonucleic acid. Although the blueprints differ across life-forms—after all, plants, fungi, and animals are very different organisms—the way it is encoded in DNA is identical.

The DNA molecule encodes all information using four chemical bases: cytosine (C), guanine (G), adenine (A) and thymine (T). It has two complementary strands, each with a long sugar-phosphate backbone to which the four chemicals attach. The sequence or order of these chemicals contains the data to develop, maintain and grow the organism. In DNA, these four chemicals always link together the same way to form pairs: A pairs with T; C pairs with G. In this very specific way, the two complementary strands link together to form DNA: a long molecule that looks a little like a rope ladder—only about 200 million times smaller! Give the "ladder" a clockwise twist, and you can see why DNA is also called the "double helix."

When organisms grow, their cells divide and in almost all cases each cell receives a duplicate of the DNA molecule. DNA's ingenious structure allows for easy replication: Each strand of the double helix contains all the information needed to create a new DNA molecule. If the pairs let go of each other, each backbone with its sequence of four chemicals can be the bases of a new DNA molecule. As A and T always pair up and C and G also always go together, one strand is enough to re-create the molecule.

MATERIALS

Tape, about 0.8 inch (2 cm) wide and 4.9 feet (1.5 m) long (such as painter's tape)
Card stock or sturdy paper
Red, yellow, blue, and green markers
Ruler

Pencil
Scissors
A partner
Blanket or sheets of paper
Rope or thick string about 3.3 feet (1 m) long (optional)

PREPARATION

- Cut 40 strips out of paper, 1.6 inches (4 cm) by 0.4 inch (1 cm) each. Divide each strip with a pencil line so it consists of two rectangles that are 0.8 inch (2 cm) by 0.4 inch (1 cm) each. These rectangles represent the bases or code chemicals of your DNA.

- There are only four different bases or code chemicals in DNA. We will use color to indicate each one: red, yellow, blue, and green. These code chemicals are very particular—red only combines with yellow, and blue only with green. Color the strips on either side of the dividing line so you have red-yellow and blue-green strips. Color them identically front and back. (Note that in your body these base pairs are tiny and not colorful! We have made them large and colorful, so the model is beautiful and easier to understand. Your DNA has a length of about 3 billion base pairs, so you will only model a piece of DNA—not the whole sequence!) This activity makes one model of a piece of DNA.

- DNA looks like a twisted rope ladder. For your model you will first make the "backbone" sides of the ladder and then add the "base pair" rungs. Start by cutting two pieces of tape, each 2 feet (0.6 m) long. Lay them parallel to each other on the table, sticky side up, with about 0.8 inch (2 cm) of space in between. Use short pieces of tape to keep the two backbones in place while you add the base pairs.

PROCEDURE

- Pick a prepared strip of paper (a base pair) and stick one end to one backbone and the other end to the other parallel backbone. The strip should make a nice bridge from one backbone to the other and cross the backbones at a right angle, just like the rungs on a rope ladder. Note your strips will not reach across the full width of both strips of tape but start and end near the middle of the pieces of tape.

- Stick more strips to the backbones so they make parallel rungs. Leave about 0.4 inch (1 cm) of space between rungs. Do this until your backbones are connected by base pairs from one end to the other.

- Remove the pieces of tape securing the backbones to the table and fold each line of tape over lengthwise in the middle. The tape will fold over the ends of the base pairs, fixing them between the folded pieces of tape.

- Your model is almost finished! One detail is missing: DNA is twisted. Hold one end of your ladder and have your partner hold the other end. Twist your end clockwise a few times. *What happens to the length of your DNA piece when you twist it? Do you see why DNA is called a double helix?*

- DNA can duplicate itself using the information contained in either strand. *Do you think you can do the same with your DNA molecule?*

- To test whether you can, untwist your DNA model and lay it flat on a table or the ground. Hide one strand with paper or a blanket. Your job is to use the knowledge you gained while making the DNA molecule to complete the molecule. *For each visible color (code chemical) can you tell which color (code chemical) is hidden? How could this help you duplicate your DNA molecule?*

ExTRA

Cut each base pair just where the two colors—each representing one code chemical—meet. Now, use each strand to duplicate the original DNA model. *Do you get two identical molecules?*

OBSERVATIONS AND RESULTS ·········

You were most likely able to tell what the hidden colors were—no matter which strand you chose to hide. This is because once you know one side of a pair you know its partner, because these chemicals always pair with the same partner: red with blue; green with yellow.

The four code chemicals in real DNA are usually represented by the letters T, A, C, and G. They are not colorful, but they are as particular: T and A always pair together, as do G and C. The sequence along one backbone of the DNA molecule contains all the information to re-create the molecule.

You probably have about 30 base pairs in your model. You would need to make it 100 million times longer to model all 3 billion base pairs of human DNA. Your model would be about 37,300 miles, or 60,000 kilometers, long—about 1.5 times around the world! Your DNA molecule is probably about 1.6 inches (4 cm) wide. Real DNA is about 2 nanometers, or 2 millionths of a millimeter wide. This means your model is about 20 million times wider than real DNA. This long string of DNA is coiled and folded into the center of almost every cell of the human body!

CLEANUP ··

Recycle the paper strips and put away all supplies.

13

Floating Arms

FEEL YOUR ARMS FLOAT ON THEIR OWN—WITH THIS FUN PHYSIOLOGICAL TRICK!

Have you ever wondered how a decision to move your arm can make your arm move? When your brain creates a command to move your arm, nerves pass along the command and muscles in the arm contract as ordered. These muscle contractions make your arm move. But could your arm move without a command from the brain? This activity is a fun and surprising way to find out!

PROJECT TIME
5 minutes

KEY CONCEPTS
Biology
Muscles
Movement
Nervous system

15

BACKGROUND

Contractions of muscles create bodily movements. More specifically, skeletal muscles, or the muscles attached to our bones, help us move our bodies—and even swallow and sneeze! Most of the time skeletal muscles contract on command—the brain produces the order, which the nerves convey, and the muscles execute. We call these voluntary contractions, or voluntary movements.

Occasionally skeletal muscles contract without an order from the brain. We call these involuntary muscle contractions. When your fingers touch something hot you automatically pull your arm back before even realizing you touched something hot. A sneeze is another example. These involuntary muscle contractions are helpful and protect us from harm. But some involuntary muscle contractions such as spasms are less desirable.

Sometimes the brain can suppress or override an involuntary muscle contraction. You might become aware of an impending sneeze and be able to suppress it or you might deliberately touch something hot, and your brain will order your arm to stay extended before you feel the pain. Neuroscientists are researching how this mechanism works. Does the brain order the muscles to extend when the involuntary signal was to contract, or block the involuntary contraction signal before it reaches the muscles?

The involuntary muscle contraction explored in this activity is known as the Kohnstamm phenomenon. It was first described in 1915 and occurs when we have voluntarily contracted a skeletal muscle for an extended period of time. Try it out—and see how your arm seems to have a will of its own!

MATERIALS

- Open doorway

PREPARATION

- Stand inside the doorway looking straight ahead into the room. Lift both arms until the backs of your hands are pressed against the door frame. If you have a shorter arm span, you might need to push with just one arm against the door frame.

- In a moment you will press the backs of your hands against the door frame while you count slowly to 60. Then you will stop pushing, step out of the doorway, relax your arms, and observe. *How do you expect your arms to feel just after you have stopped pushing?*

PROCEDURE

- Try it out! Push for about a minute, step away and relax your arms. *How do your arms feel? Do you observe anything unexpected?* If nothing surprising happened, try again. This time try to press the backs of your hands a little harder against the door frame for a full minute. After that, step out of the doorway, relax your arms, and observe. *Do you feel your arms floating up all by themselves?*

- Do the test again, but try to keep your arms down pointing to the ground after you walk out of the doorway. *Can you do it? How does it feel?*

- *Do you think you can make one arm float up by only pushing the door frame with one hand?* Try it out and feel for yourself!

- *Do you think you need to push for a full minute or would half a minute or a few seconds be enough?* Try a few times and see if you can find the minimum time required.

- *Do you think you need to push hard against the doorway for your arms to float up or would a gentle push be fine, too?* Try it and see how it feels.

ExTRA

See what happens when you rotate your hands and push with the insides of your hands up against the door frame. *Do you feel different muscles working now? How do your arms feel when you walk out of the doorway?*

17

ExTRA

Can you make your leg float up after pushing it sideways against the wall?

ExTRA

Press the backs of your hands against the door frame for about one minute, then step out but deliberately keep your arms down for a few seconds before relaxing them. *Do they still float up? How long do you need to counteract the phenomenon for it to disappear?*

OBSERVATIONS AND RESULTS ···········

Could you see and feel your arms float up when you walked out of the doorway? After you voluntarily contracted specific arm muscles for a minute or so, they contracted by themselves. You were probably able to counteract this to keep your arms down, but it took effort to do so.

If you tried, you could probably make it happen with just one arm, too. You might have discovered you need to push for an extended time—and quite hard—before the muscles contract all by themselves once you have stopped pushing. Scientists know these spontaneous contractions, known as the Kohnstamm phenomenon, are due to involuntary orders sent by the brain. They are less sure about why these occur.

Researchers also have found the brain blocks the involuntary orders to suppress the Kohnstamm phenomenon. When you try to keep your arms down after you prompt the phenomenon, your brain does not order your arms to extend to counteract the contraction. Instead, it blocks the spontaneous order to contract the muscles.

It is important for scientists to understand the mechanisms by which the body produces and suppresses spontaneous contractions, because this knowledge might help people, such as those afflicted with Parkinson's disease, who experience illness-induced spontaneous contractions.

CLEANUP ························

There is no cleanup for this experiment.

Exploring Enzymes

READY, SET, REACT! LEARN HOW ENZYMES POWER EVERYTHING FROM OUR DIGESTION TO PROTECTING OUR CELLS FROM DAMAGE, AND WATCH THEM IN ACTION IN THIS ACTIVITY.

PROJECT TIME

20 minutes

KEY CONCEPTS
Biology
Biochemistry
Enzymes
Physiology
Chemistry

Have you ever wondered how all the food that you eat gets digested? It is not only the acid in your stomach that breaks down your food—many little molecules in your body, called enzymes, help with that too. Enzymes are special types of proteins that speed up chemical reactions, such as the digestion of food in your stomach. In fact, there are thousands of different enzymes in your body that work around-the-clock to keep you healthy and active. In this science activity you will investigate one of these enzymes, called catalase, to find out how it helps to protect your body from damage.

19

BACKGROUND

Enzymes are essential for our survival. These proteins, made by our cells, help transform chemicals in our body, functioning as a catalyst. A catalyst gets reactions started and makes them happen faster, by increasing the rate of a reaction that otherwise might not happen at all or would take too long to sustain life. However, a catalyst does not take part in the reaction itself—so how does this work? Each chemical reaction needs a minimum amount of energy to make it happen. This energy is called the activation energy. The lower the activation energy of a reaction, the faster it takes place. If the activation energy is too high, the reaction does not occur.

Enzymes have the ability to lower the activation energy of a chemical reaction by interacting with its reactants (the chemicals doing the reacting). Each enzyme has an active site, which is where the reaction takes place. These sites are like special pockets that are able to bind a chemical molecule. The compounds or molecules the enzyme reacts with are called their substrates. The enzyme pocket has a special shape so that only one specific substrate is able to bind to it, just like only one key fits into a specific lock. Once the molecule is bound to the enzyme, the chemical reaction takes place. Then, the reaction products are released from the pocket, and the enzyme is ready to start all over again with another substrate molecule.

Catalase is a very common enzyme that is present in almost all organisms that are exposed to oxygen. The purpose of catalase in living cells is to protect them from oxidative damage, which can occur when cells or other molecules in the body come into contact with oxidative compounds. This damage is a natural result of reactions happening inside your cells. The reactions can include by-products such as hydrogen peroxide, which can be harmful to the body, just as how a by-product of a nice bonfire can be unwanted smoke that makes you cough or stings your eyes. To prevent such damage, the catalase enzyme helps get rid of these compounds by breaking up hydrogen peroxide (H_2O_2) into harmless water and oxygen. Do you want to see the catalyze enzyme in action? In this activity you will disarm hydrogen peroxide with the help of catalase from yeast.

MATERIALS

- Safety goggles or protective glasses

- 5 teaspoons (24 ml) of dish soap

- One package of dry yeast
- Hydrogen peroxide, 3 percent (at least 1/2 cup [118 ml])
- 3 tablespoons
- 1 teaspoon
- five 16-ounce disposable plastic cups
- Tap water
- Measuring cup
- Permanent marker
- Paper towel
- Workspace that can get wet (and won't be damaged by any spilled hydrogen peroxide or food-colored water)
- Food coloring (optional)

PREPARATION ·······································

- Take one cup and dissolve the dry yeast in about 1/2 cup (118 ml) of warm tap water. The water shouldn't be too hot but close to body temperature (98.6°F, or 37°C). Let the dissolved yeast rest for at least five minutes.

- Use the permanent marker to label the remaining four cups from 1 to 4.

- To all the labeled cups, add 1 teaspoon (19.7 ml) of dish soap.

- To cup 1 no further additions are made at this point.

- Before using the hydrogen peroxide, put on your safety goggles to protect your eyes. In case you spill hydrogen peroxide, clean it up with a wet paper towel. If you get it on your skin, make sure to rinse the affected area with plenty of water.

- To cup 2, add 1 tablespoon (15 ml) of 3 percent hydrogen peroxide solution. Use a fresh spoon for the hydrogen peroxide.

- To cup 3, add 2 tablespoons (30 ml) of the hydrogen peroxide.

- To cup four, add 3 tablespoons (45 ml) of the hydrogen peroxide.

- Optionally, you can add a drop of food color to each of the labeled cups. (You can choose a different color for each one for easy identification.)

PROCEDURE

- Take cup number 1 and place it in front of you on the work area. With a fresh tablespoon, add 1 tablespoon (15 ml) of the dissolved yeast solution to the cup and swirl it slightly. *What happens after you add the yeast? Do you see a reaction happening?*

- Place cup number 2 in front of you and again add 1 tablespoon (15 ml) of yeast solution to the cup. *Once you add the enzyme, does the catalase react with the hydrogen peroxide? Can you see the reaction products being formed?*

- Add 1 tablespoon (15 ml) of yeast solution to cup number 3. *Do you see the same reaction taking place? Is the result different or the same compared to cup number two?*

- Finally, add 1 tablespoon (15 ml) of yeast solution to cup number 4. *Do you see more or less reaction products compared to your previous results? Can you explain the difference?*

- Place all 4 cups next to each other in front of you and observe your results. *Did the enzymatic reaction take place in all of the cups or was there an exception? How do the results in each cup look different? Why do you think this is the case?*

- Now, take cup number 1 and add one additional tablespoon (15 ml) of 3 percent hydrogen peroxide to the cup. Swirl the cup slightly to mix the solution. *What happens now? Looking at all your results, what do you think is the limiting factor for the catalase reaction in your cups?*

EXTRA

Repeat this activity, but this time do not add dish soap to all of the reactions. *What is different once you remove the dish soap? Do you still see foam formation?*

EXTRA

So far you have observed the effect of substrate (H_2O_2) concentration on the catalase reaction. *What happens if you keep the substrate concentration constant but change the concentration of the enzyme?* Try adding different amounts of yeast solution to 3 tablespoons (45 ml) of hydrogen peroxide, starting with 1 teaspoon. *Do you observe any differences, or does the concentration of catalase not matter in your reaction?*

EXTRA

What happens if the environmental conditions for the enzyme are changed? Repeat the catalase reaction, but this time vary conditions such as the pH by adding vinegar (an acid) or baking soda (a base) or change the reaction temperature by heating the solution in the microwave. *Can you identify which conditions are optimal for the catalase reaction? Are there any conditions that eliminate the catalase activity?*

SCIENCE FAIR IDEA

Can you find other sources of catalase enzyme that you could use in this activity? Research what other organisms, plants, or cells contain catalase and try using these for your reaction. *Do they work as well as yeast?*

OBSERVATIONS AND RESULTS ·········

You probably saw lots of bubbles and foam in this activity. What made the foam appear? When the enzyme catalase comes into contact with its substrate, hydrogen peroxide, it starts breaking it down into water and oxygen. Oxygen is a gas and therefore wants to escape the liquid. However, the dish soap that you added to all your solutions is able to trap the gas bubbles, which results in the formation of a stable foam. As long as there is enzyme and hydrogen peroxide present in the solution, the reaction continues, and foam is produced. Once one of both compounds is depleted, the product formation stops. If you do not add dish soap to the reaction, you will see bubbles generated but no stable foam formation.

If there is no hydrogen peroxide present, the catalase cannot function, which is why in cup 1 you shouldn't have seen any bubble or foam production. Only when hydrogen peroxide is available, the catalase reaction can take place as you probably observed in the other cups. In fact, the catalase reaction is dependent on the substrate concentration. If you have an excess of enzyme but not enough substrate, the reaction will be limited by the substrate availability. Once you add more hydrogen peroxide to the solution, the reaction rate will increase as more substrate molecules can collide with the enzyme, forming more product. The result is an increasing amount of foam produced in your cup as you increase the amount of H_2O_2 in your reaction. You should have seen more foam being produced once you added another tablespoon of hydrogen peroxide to cup 1, which should have resulted in a similar amount of foam as in cup 2. However, at some point you will reach a substrate concentration at which the enzyme gets saturated and becomes the limiting factor. In this case, you have to add more enzyme to speed up the reaction again.

Many other factors affect the activity of enzymes as well. Most enzymes only function under optimal environmental conditions. If the pH or temperature deviates from these conditions too much, the enzyme reaction slows down significantly or does not work at all. You might have noticed that when doing the extra steps in the procedure.

CLEANUP ·

Pour all the solutions into the sink and clean all the spoons with warm water and dish soap. Wipe your work area with a wet paper towel and wash your hands with water and soap.

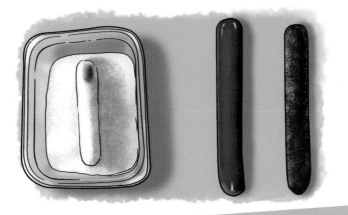

Sarcophagus Science
Mummify a Hot Dog

TURN A HOT DOG INTO A MUMMY USING BAKING SODA...
BUT DON'T WORRY! THIS MUMMY ISN'T SCARY!

Mummies are frequently featured in movies and television shows—often playing the part of a scary, undead monster. But in ancient Egypt and in other cultures, mummification was a serious religious burial ritual. In this activity, you will learn about the science behind the process of mummification by mummifying a hot dog.

PROJECT TIME
20 minutes to set up, weeks to embalm your hot dog

KEY CONCEPTS
Human biology
Water
Mummification
Desiccation
Decomposition

BACKGROUND

A mummy is a corpse—human or other animal—whose tissue has been preserved, whether intentionally by a process developed by humans or in nature by an accident of chemistry or weather. Ancient Egyptians believed that preserving the body was an important preparation for one's afterlife. The oldest evidence of Egyptians performing mummification dates to about 3500 BCE (although older purposefully mummified remains have been found elsewhere, such as ones dating to about 5050 BCE in Chile). We have also learned a lot about early animals and humans from individuals that were naturally preserved, thanks to a fluke burial in sediment or ice.

There were several steps to the Egyptian ritual of mummification that were important for preserving a body: after thoroughly washing it in the waters of the nearby Nile River, specialists would remove several internal organs from the body. This was important because internal organs are some of the first bodily parts to decompose. The body would then be stuffed and covered with natron to desiccate it (or dry it out). Natron is a naturally occurring salt mixture that includes baking soda (sodium bicarbonate). Once desiccated (dried out), the body was rubbed with perfumed oils and then carefully wrapped with linen bandages. The remains were then placed inside of a sarcophagus, which was in turn placed inside a tomb. In this activity, you'll get to play embalmer and mummify a hot dog using baking soda.

MATERIALS

- Disposable gloves (optional)
- Meat hot dog
- Paper towels
- Ruler
- Piece of string or yarn
- Scrap piece of paper and pen or pencil
- Airtight plastic storage box with lid that is longer, wider, and much deeper than the hot dog
- Approximately 6 pounds (2.7 kg) of fresh baking soda. You will need enough to thoroughly surround and cover the hot dog in the box twice.

PREPARATION ·

- Place the hot dog on top of a paper towel on a counter or other hard surface. If you want to, you can wear disposable gloves while handling the hot dog.

- Observe the hot dog. *How does it look and smell?*

- Measure the length of the hot dog and its circumference. (Measure its circumference by wrapping the string around the hot dog and then laying that length of the string up next to the ruler.) Write these measurements down.

- If you do not wear gloves while handling the hot dog, be sure to thoroughly wash your hands after handling it.

PROCEDURE ·

- Put at least 1 inch (2.5 cm) of baking soda (from a new, unopened box) in the bottom of the storage box. Lay the hot dog flat on top of the baking soda. Cover the hot dog with at least 1 more inch (2.5 cm) of baking soda, making sure the hot dog has baking soda along its sides and is completely covered on top.

- Seal the box with its lid and put it in an indoor shady location away from heating and cooling vents where it will not be disturbed. It should remain undisturbed for one week.

- After one week check on the hot dog. You may use gloves to handle it or wash your hands afterward. Gently tap and dust all of the baking soda off of the hot dog and into a trash can. *How does the hot dog look and smell now?*

- Place the hot dog on a paper towel and measure its length and circumference. Write these measurements down. *Has the length or circumference changed?*

27

Discard the old baking soda and clean out the box. Make sure you dry it thoroughly. Again, from a fresh box, put at least 1 inch (2.5 cm) of baking soda in the bottom of the storage box. Lay the hot dog flat on top of the baking soda and then cover it with at least 1 more inch (2.5 cm), making sure there's baking soda along its sides and completely covering it on top.

Seal the box again and put it back in the location where it was before. It should remain undisturbed for one more week.

After the week has passed, check on the hot dog. Gently tap and dust all the baking soda off of the hot dog and into a trash can. *How does the hot dog look and smell now? How is its condition different from that of the first day, and after being mummified for just one week?*

Place the hot dog on a paper towel and measure its length and circumference. *How have the measurements changed compared with the first day and after just one week of mummification? What do you think this tells you about the mummification process?*

ExTRA

Try this activity with different varieties of hot dogs. *Do chicken hot dogs mummify faster than beef hot dogs? What about hot dogs made with a variety of meats?*

ExTRA

If you saw a big difference in the hot dog at two weeks compared with one week, then the hot dog may still only be partially mummified. You could continue to mummify it, adding fresh baking soda and recording measurements and observations once a week for a few weeks until you do not see any more changes. *How long do you need to repeat this mummification process until the hot dog is completely mummified?*

SCIENCE FAIR IDEA

Investigate the different ways that ancient people mummified human remains and/or how living things have been naturally preserved (such as with the bog bodies found in northern Europe or even a mummified dinosaur that was discovered in North Dakota). *How could you apply any of these techniques to mummifying a hot dog?*

OBSERVATIONS AND RESULTS · · · · · · · · ·

After one week of mummification, did the hot dog look darker in color, smell bad and shrink slightly? After two weeks, did the hot dog look about the same and shrink only a tiny bit more, if at all?

Baking soda is a desiccant, which is a substance that dries out things close to it. It does this by absorbing moisture from its surrounding environment. The baking soda should have absorbed the moisture from the hot dog, desiccating (drying) it. (Fresh baking soda is needed because older baking soda will probably not be as effective, having already absorbed moisture from its surrounding environment.) As the hot dog lost moisture, it changed color, smelled bad, and shrank, with the most significant changes (and moisture loss) being observed after one week and only smaller (if any) changes after two weeks total. For example, you may have seen that the hot dog became about 4 percent shorter and 25 percent smaller in circumference after one week, and about 6 percent shorter and only 27 percent smaller in circumference after two weeks total compared with its original condition. It may not have noticeably changed in color or smell after two weeks compared with its condition after the first week.

CLEANUP · · · · · · · · · · · ·

Do not eat the mummified hot dog! It can be disposed of in the trash.

Sweaty Science

How Does Heart Rate Change with Exercise?

WE ALL KNOW THAT EXERCISE IS IMPORTANT, BUT DO YOU KNOW HOW EXERCISE AFFECTS YOUR HEART? TRY THIS EXPERIMENT TO FIND OUT!

Have you ever wondered how many times your heart beats in a day, a month, a year—or will beat in total throughout your life? Over an average lifetime, the human heart beats more than 2.5 billion times. For a person to keep their heart healthy, they should eat right, not smoke, and get regular exercise. In this science activity, you'll measure your heart rate during different types of physical activities to find out which gives your heart the best workout to help keep it fit.

PROJECT TIME

30 minutes

KEY CONCEPTS

The heart
Heart rate
Health
Exercise

31

BACKGROUND

A 150-pound (68 kg) adult has about 5.8 quarts (5.5 l) of blood on average, which the heart circulates about three times every minute. A person's heart is continuously beating to keep the blood circulating. Heart health experts say that the best ways to keep our hearts healthy is through a balanced diet, avoiding smoking, and regular exercise.

Exercise that is good for your heart should elevate your heart rate. But by how much, for how long, and how often should your heart rate be elevated? This has to do with how fit you are and your maximum heart rate, which, for adults, is about 220 beats per minute (bpm) minus your age. For example, if you are 30 years old, your maximum heart rate would be 190 bpm. The American Heart Association (AHA) recommends doing exercise that increases a person's heart rate to between 50 to 85 percent of their maximum heart rate. This range is called the target heart rate zone. The AHA recommends a person gets at least 30 minutes of moderate to vigorous exercise—exercise that elevates their heart rate to the target heart rate zone—on most days of the week, or a total of about 150 minutes a week.

MATERIALS

- Scrap piece of paper
- Pen or pencil
- Clock or timer that shows seconds or a helper with a watch
- Comfortable exercise clothes (optional)
- Simple and fun exercise equipment, such as a jump rope, bicycle, Hula-Hoop, 2-pound (0.9 kg) weight, etc.

Alternatively, you can do exercises that do not require equipment, such as walking, doing jumping jacks, jogging in place, etc. You will want to do at least two different types of exercises, both of which you can sustain for 15 minutes. (Remember to always stop an exercise if you feel faint.)
- Calculator

PREPARATION ·······························

- Practice finding your pulse. Use the first two fingers of one hand to feel your radial pulse on the opposite wrist. You should find your radial pulse on the "thumb side" of your wrist, just below the base of your hand. Practice finding your pulse until you can do it quickly. (You can alternatively take your carotid pulse to do this activity but be sure you know how to safely take it and press on your neck only very lightly with your fingers.)

- Measure your resting heart rate, which is your heart rate when you are awake but relaxed, such as when you have been lying still for several minutes. To do this, take your pulse when you have been resting and multiply the number of beats you count in 10 seconds by six. This will give you your resting heart rate in beats per minute (bpm). *What is your resting heart rate?* Write it on a scrap piece of paper.

- You will be measuring your heart rate during different types of physical exercises over a period of 15 minutes. Choose at least two different exercises. Some examples include jumping rope, lifting a 2-pound (0.9 kg) weight, riding a bike, Hula-Hooping, walking, etc. Gather any needed materials. *Do you think the activities will affect your heart rate differently? How do you think doing each activity will affect your heart rate?*

PROCEDURE ·······························

- Choose which exercise you want to do first. Before starting it, make sure you have been resting for a few minutes so that your heart is at its resting heart rate.

- Perform the first exercise for 15 minutes. While you do this, write down the number of beats you count in 10 seconds after 1, 2, 5, 10, and 15 minutes of activity. (You want to quickly check your pulse because it can start to slow within 15 seconds of stopping exercising.) *How do the number of beats you count change over time? How did you feel by the end of the exercise?*

33

- Calculate your heart rate after 1, 2, 5, 10, and 15 minutes of exercise by multiplying the number of beats you counted (in 10 seconds) by six. *How did your heart rate (in bpm) change over time?*

- Repeat this process for at least one other exercise. Leave enough time between the exercises so that your heart rate returns to around its normal resting level (this should only take a few minutes). *How did you feel by the end of the second exercise? How did your heart rate change over time for this exercise?*

- Take a look at the results you wrote down for this activity. *Which exercise increased your heart rate the most? Which exercise increased your heart rate the fastest? Which exercise(s) elevated your heart rate to the target heart rate zone (50 to 85 percent of your maximum heart rate, where your maximum heart rate is 220 bpm minus your age)? Do you notice any consistent patterns in your results?*

SCIENCE FAIR IDEA

Try this activity again, but test different physical exercises. *How does your heart rate change when you do other exercises? How are the changes similar and how are they different?*

EXTRA

Measure your heart rate while lying down, while sitting down, and while standing. *How does your heart rate change with body position?*

EXTRA

Repeat this activity with other healthy volunteers. *How does their heart rate compare to yours? How does their change in heart rate while exercising compare to how yours changed?*

EXTRA

Try this activity again but vary the intensity of your exercise. *What intensity level elevates your heart rate to 50 percent of its maximum heart rate? What about nearly 85 percent of its maximum?* Be sure not to exceed your recommended target heart rate zone while exercising!

OBSERVATIONS AND RESULTS ·········

After just a minute of exercise, did you see your heart rate reach its target heart rate zone? Did it initially jump higher for a more strenuous exercise, like Hula-Hooping, compared to a more moderately intense exercise, such as walking?

If you did a moderately intense exercise, such as walking, you may have seen an initial jump in your heart rate (where your heart rate falls within the lower end of your target heart rate zone within about one minute of exercise), but then your heart rate only slowly increased after that. After 15 minutes, you may have reached the middle of your target heart rate zone. To reach the upper end, people usually need to do a moderately intense exercise for a longer amount of time (such as for 30 minutes). If you did a more strenuous exercise—Hula-Hooping, for example— you may have seen a higher initial bump in your heart rate (such as reaching the middle of your target heart rate zone after just one minute of exercise), and then your heart rate stayed about the same for the remaining 14 minutes of exercise. Overall, doing a more strenuous exercise generally raises a person's heart rate faster compared to doing an exercise that is only moderately intense.

CLEANUP ··

Return all materials to the place where you found them.

Stepping Science
Estimating Someone's Height from Their Walk

CAN YOU MEASURE HOW TALL YOU ARE BY WALKING?
TRY THIS EASY EXPERIMENT TO FIND OUT!

Do you ever find that you need to walk faster to keep up with some people whereas you have to decrease your pace to walk with others? This is likely because of the difference in leg length between you and the person you are walking with. In this science activity, you'll get to investigate just how much faster or slower different people walk and see if you can use the relationship between a person's walking pace and their height to estimate your own height.

PROJECT TIME
15 minutes

KEY CONCEPTS
Height
Distance
Walking
Estimation

37

BACKGROUND

A pedometer is an instrument that is often used by joggers and walkers to tell them how far a distance they have gone. On some pedometers, when a person sets the instrument to record an outing, they must enter their height into the pedometer to get an accurate reading.

Why is height an important variable for measuring how far a person has walked? One part of the answer has to do with ratios. Our bodies have many interesting ratios. For example, when your arms are outstretched, the distance from the tip of one hand to the other is usually about equal to your height. There are other ratios as well, each describing how one part of the body relates to another in size. Because the length of a person's legs is related to their height by a ratio, the latter will affect how long of a step they take. The longer each step, the more distance a person travels when taking the same number of steps while walking, jogging, or running. This ratio, combined with the motions involved in walking and running, is used by pedometers to calculate traversed distances.

MATERIALS

20 feet (6.1 m) of straight sidewalk or hallway
Sidewalk chalk or two small objects to mark off 20 feet (6.1 m) of distance
Tape measure

At least three volunteers to walk a short distance (Ideally, they should be different heights.)
Pen or pencil
Scrap piece of paper
Calculator

PREPARATION

- Find a place that has 20 feet (6.1 m) of straight sidewalk or find a straight hallway that is at least 20 feet (6.1 m) long.

- Using a tape measure, measure out a distance of 20 feet (6.1 m) and mark the beginning and end points with a piece of sidewalk chalk (if you are using a sidewalk) or mark them each with small objects that will not be moved (if you are using an indoor hallway).

PROCEDURE

- Measure a volunteer's height. *How tall are they?* Write their height down on a scrap piece of paper.

- Ask the volunteer to walk from the beginning to the end of the 20-foot (6.1 m) course you marked at a normal pace and stride. As they do, count the number of steps they take. *How many steps did you count?* Write down the answer.

- Repeat this process for at least two more volunteers. *How tall is each volunteer? Did they take a similar number of steps or was there variation?* Be sure to write the results down.

- For each volunteer, figure out their step length (in feet) by dividing 20 feet (6.1 m) by the number of steps each took. *What was the step length for each volunteer?*

- For each volunteer, figure out their ratio of step length to height by dividing their step length by their height (both in feet). *What numbers do you get for this ratio? Are they similar for the different volunteers or is there variation?* Average the step length to height ratio for all of your volunteers. Be sure to write your answers down.

- Lastly, use your results to estimate your own height. Walk from one end to the other of your 20-foot (6.1 m) course while counting the number of steps you take. Divide 20 feet (6.1 m) by the number of steps you took. *What was your step length?* Then divide your step length by the volunteers' average ratio of step length to height. *Based on your data, what is your estimated height?*

- Have someone measure your actual height. *How does your actual height compare with your estimated height? How accurate was your estimate?*

EXTRA ~~~~~~~~~~~~~~~~~~~~

Try this activity with a greater number of people. For example, you could go to a park with a jogging path or a similar location with an adult where you can ask for volunteers as they pass by. Try to collect data from at least 10 volunteers. *Is there much variation in the ratio of step length to height when comparing many people? Does collecting more data make your height estimation more accurate?*

EXTRA ~~~~~~~~~~~~~~~~~~~~

You could do this activity again, but this time have volunteers walk slowly, moderately fast, or very fast. *How does a person's speed affect their step length?*

EXTRA ~~~~~~~~~~~~~~~~~~~~

The human body has many other interesting ratios, such as those mentioned in the Background section of this activity. You could look into other ratios in the human body and come up with an activity like this one to investigate them. *What other ratios are consistently found in the human body from person to person?*

OBSERVATIONS AND RESULTS ··········

When you divided your volunteers' step lengths by their heights, did you get a ratio value close to 0.4? Were you able to roughly estimate your height based on this, accurate to within a couple inches?

The measurements of a pedometer are based on the hypothesis that all people have common ratios and proportions, even if they are different heights. In this activity you should have found this hypothesis to be pretty accurate. On average, adults have a step length of about 2.2 to 2.5 feet (0.7 to 0.8 m). In general, if you divide a person's step length by their height, the ratio value you get is about 0.4 (with a range from about 0.41 to 0.45). This is why you can take a person's step length and divide it by about 0.43 to roughly estimate their height—the estimated height will likely be within 2 inches (5 cm) of (and probably much closer to) their actual height.

CLEANUP ·

Return any materials to the place where you found them.

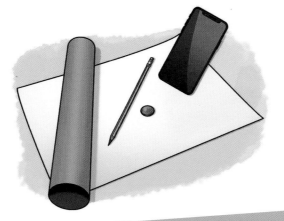

Side-Dominant Science
Are You Left- or Right-Sided?

YOU PROBABLY KNOW IF YOU ARE LEFT- OR RIGHT-HANDED, BUT DO YOU KNOW IF THAT EXTENDS TO THE REST OF YOUR BODY? FIND OUT WITH THIS SIMPLE EXPERIMENT.

If you write with your right hand, you might also prefer to draw a picture, throw a ball, or eat food with the same hand. But have you ever wondered if your right foot is also more dominant than your left foot? What about your right eye and ear—do you prefer to use them more than your left ones? In this activity, you'll get to find out whether people have a sidedness—that is, whether they generally prefer to do most activities with one side of their body—and which side that is.

PROJECT TIME
40 minutes

KEY CONCEPTS
Brain
Laterality
Handedness
Sidedness
Left/right dominance

43

BACKGROUND

Each person's brain is divided into two sides—the left and right hemispheres. In some cases, one hemisphere may be more active than the other during a certain activity. For example, when someone processes language, one hemisphere is usually more active than the other. Doing this or other activities, however, is not absolutely limited to using one hemisphere or the other, or even certain hemispheric parts. Different brain areas are important and work together for different activities, such as speech, hearing, and sight. But if part of a hemisphere is damaged when a person is young, other parts of the brain can often take over doing whatever the damaged regions of the brain used to do.

What do the brain's hemispheres have to do with sidedness? When someone is processing language, one hemisphere is usually working harder than the other. There is also some correlation between the side(s) we use in our brain and the side we use on our body. This preference to use one side of the body over the other is known as sidedness, laterality, or left/right dominance.

MATERIALS

- Paper
- Pen or pencil
- A coin

- Paper towel tube or toilet paper tube
- A seashell or phone
- At least five volunteers

PREPARATION

- Have all of the materials ready so that you will be able to quickly test each volunteer.

- Prepare a small data table on a piece of paper to record your results. Going down the left side of the paper, write: "Hand," "Foot," "Eye," and "Ear." Going across the top of the paper, write your volunteers' names.

PROCEDURE

- Ask your first volunteer to write their name on a piece of paper. *Which hand do they write their name with?* Record the result (writing either "Right" or "Left") in your data table in the row labeled "Hand" in the column under the volunteer's name.

- Place a coin on the floor directly in front of your first volunteer. Ask them to step onto the coin. *Which foot is used to step on the coin?* Record the result in your data table in the "Foot" row, under the volunteer's name.

- Give your first volunteer a paper towel tube or toilet paper tube and ask them to look at a distant object through it. *Which eye do they use to look through the tube?* Record the result in your data table in the "Eye" row, under the volunteer's name.

- Give your first volunteer a seashell or phone and ask them to listen to it. *Which ear do they put the shell or phone up to?* Record the result in your data table in the "Ear" column, under the volunteer's name.

- Repeat this process with at least four other volunteers. Be sure to record the results under the volunteers' name each time.

- *Are more of your volunteers right-handed or left-handed? What about right-footed versus left-footed, right-eyed versus left-eyed, and right-eared versus left-eared? What side is the most common overall?*

- *How many right-handed people are also right-footed? (How about for lefties?) What about for the other possible combinations? Do you see a correlation?*

EXTRA

In this activity you only used one test to check for dominance in your volunteer's hands, feet, eyes, and ears. Using additional tests would help you check and confirm your results. *Can you think of other ways to test for sidedness using objects from around your home? Using other tests, are the results the same as the ones you got doing the original activity?*

OBSERVATIONS AND RESULTS

Were more of your volunteers right-handed than left-handed? If a person was right-handed, did they usually also use their right foot, eye, and ear?

You probably already know that most people are right-handed. In fact, roughly 70 to 90 percent of people are right-handed. From this activity, you probably saw that most people who are right-handed are also right-sided overall. That is, they mostly prefer to use their right foot, eye, and ear as well. But there are certainly exceptions, particularly with eyes and ears—a right-handed person may prefer using their right foot and right ear but prefer their left eye over their right one. Similarly, a right-handed person may prefer their right foot and eye but prefer their left ear. You may have seen a similar trend with left-handed people. Because the majority of people who are right-handed are also right-footed, in some cases where a person writes with their right hand but prefers to use their left foot, they may have been predisposed to being left-handed but were raised to use their right hand.

Overall, whereas the vast majority of the global population is right-handed, it's thought that a smaller percentage is right-footed, an even smaller percentage is right-eyed, and yet an even smaller percentage is right-eared (perhaps a little over half), but this trend is unlikely to be visible using only five volunteers. Why might people have a weaker preference for an eye or ear that matches their dominant side? Perhaps one ear or eye is stronger than the other.

CLEANUP

Put all materials back where you found them.

Put Your Peripheral Vision to the Test

CAN YOU SEE ME NOW? DID YOU KNOW THAT OUR CENTRAL AND SIDE VISION WORKS VERY DIFFERENTLY? LEARN HOW YOUR OWN EYES WORK TO NOTICE OBJECTS AND MOVEMENT ON THE EDGE OF YOUR VISION. YOU MAY BE SURPRISED ABOUT WHAT YOU DON'T NOTICE!

PROJECT TIME

45 minutes

KEY CONCEPTS

The human eye
Peripheral vision
Central vision

Do you only think of your peripheral (side) vision—peripherally? This side vision is actually useful for many daily activities, including riding a bike, reading, or playing basketball. You might not even realize when you are using it. But our survival once depended on the quick response of our peripheral vision. A detailed picture, created by our central vision, is only useful in situations where time allows us to focus on the details. But our side vision can help us avoid dangers quickly. In this activity, you will find out how specialized our peripheral view is.

BACKGROUND

When you look at something, you use central vision to focus on the details and peripheral vision to gather information about the surroundings.

The differences between central and peripheral vision start at the backs of our eyes where we have two types of light-sensitive cells, called cones and rods. Our central vision uses an area densely packed with cones. Cones are sensitive to color and need ample light to function well. Our peripheral vision uses mostly rods and almost no cones. Rods are sensitive to movement and quickly pick up changes in brightness. They function well in a broad range of light conditions.

The differences continue as signals travel to the brain. Some signaling cells are sensitive to color but not so much to contrast whereas other cells signal faster and respond to low-contrast stimuli. In the brain's vision center (known as the visual cortex), more neurons will analyze a stimulus picked up by our central vision compared with the same stimulus picked up by our peripheral vision. All of this leads to our color-sensitive, high-resolution central vision and our fast-working, movement-sensitive peripheral vision.

With all this information on our visual system, will you be able to predict what your side vision will perceive? Try this activity to find out!

MATERIALS

- Cardboard or foam board: One 12- by 24-inch (30- by 60-cm) board or two 12- by 12-inch (30- by 30-cm) square boards held together with tape
- A ruler
- Pencil
- A string, about 20 inches (51 cm) long
- A pushpin
- Stack of scratch paper or a newspaper
- Scissors or craft knife
- Disposable cup
- Glue or clear tape
- Construction paper or paper and markers. (We suggest red, yellow, and green but other colors work too.)
- Flat surface to hold your board
- Helper

PREPARATION

- If you have two 12- by 12-inch (30- by 30-cm) boards, tape them together so they form a 12- by 24-inch (30- by 60-cm) board.

- Place your board on a flat surface in front of you with the long side closest to you. Find the middle of the long side; this should be 12 inches (30 cm) from each corner. Mark this place with a pencil.

- Place a newspaper or stack of scratch paper under the board to protect your surface underneath and carefully stick a pushpin into the board on the indicated place.

- Tie one end of the string around the pencil. Tie the other end to the pushpin so the string is exactly 12 inches (30 cm) long.

- Use the attached pencil to draw a half circle on your board with a radius of 12 inches (30 cm).

- Shorten the string until the distance from the pencil to the pushpin is 0.8 inch (2 cm). Now draw a small half circle—within the larger circle—with a 0.8-inch (2 cm) radius.

- Remove the pencil, the string, and the pushpin and carefully use the scissors to cut along the big and small lines. (You may want help; thick cardboard or foam board can be difficult to cut.) You should be left with what looks like a rainbow. The big half circle is the outer edge of your vision protractor, the small half circle cutout makes a place for your nose.

- Pin the pushpin near the outer edge of the protractor, directly across from your nose hole. (Be sure the pin is not poking anything but the protective paper underneath.) If the protractor were a rainbow, this point would indicate the highest point of your bow. This pushpin will serve as a focus point, or a point to look at while you perform each test. (Tape some scratch paper around the point of the pushpin so it does not accidentally poke any items or people.)

- Attach a disposable cup on the bottom of the protractor, near the center. This will serve as a handle. If you started with two 12- by 12-inch (30- by 30-cm) boards, you might need to attach reinforcement on the bottom side so the two pieces of the protractor stay flat. You can use the scrap pieces of board for this.

- Your vision protractor is now ready to use.

- You now need to create some shapes to look for before you can start the test. To do so, take three different colored sheets of construction paper. We suggest trying red, green, and yellow but other colors will work, too. Cut out two 4- by 1-inch (10- by 2.5-cm) rectangular strips from each sheet, for a total of six strips. If you do not have construction paper, you can use white paper strips and color them with markers. Note that each strip needs to be one uniform color.

- Take one strip of each color and cut off the corners so the top of the strip forms a triangle. You should now have three strips like this. Leave the other three strips as rectangles.

- If your strips bend over when held up, you can reinforce them with additional paper, craft sticks or straws.

PROCEDURE

Hold the vision protractor up to your face with your nose in the center nose hole. The protractor should be held horizontally during the test, so the half-circle stretches out in front and to the side of you. Keep your gaze on the pushpin during the test.

Your helper will hold one of the paper strips against the outer edge of the vision protractor so 0.8 inch (2 cm) stick straight up above the vision board. They will hold it on your left, near the long straight edge of the protractor. While you continue looking at the pushpin, the helper will move the strip slowly and evenly along the curved protractor edge toward the middle.

How far do you think the helper will need to move the strip before you observe something is there? Do you think the helper will need to move it farther before you can detect the color and/or shape of the strip? Much farther or just a little bit?

Perform the test. As soon as you can first detect the strip, have the helper stop moving. *Can you detect the shape or the color of the object or can you just tell there is something there?* Remember to keep your eyes on the pushpin at all times during the test.

Have your helper keep moving the object along the edge toward the center of the protractor. Ask the helper to stop again as soon as you can detect more detail, such as the color or the shape. *What can you detect first—color or shape? Or are you able to detect both at the same time?*

Repeat the previous step until you can detect the shape as well as the color of the object. *Can you detect other details of the object at this location, or does it need to be moved even closer to the pushpin?*

Now let the helper choose a different strip. *Do you expect the outcome to be different? Can your peripheral vision detect one color earlier than another?*

ExTRA

Repeat the test in a darker room after allowing your eyes to adjust to the new situation. *Do you expect the results to be different and, if so, how do you expect your outcome to change?*

OBSERVATIONS AND RESULTS

You probably quickly observed something appearing in your side view but perhaps you could only later tell the color, and after that identify the shape.

Our peripheral vision is quick at detecting that something enters our field of sight, but it is weak at distinguishing color, shape, or detail. This is because fewer and different cells in our eyes and brains are activated when seeing an object with our peripheral vision than when "seeing" the object with our central vision.

Our peripheral vision has evolved to serve us well. It is very good at picking up objects and movement in dim as well as bright light, which allows us to escape from an approaching danger quickly. This explains the results of some of the extra instructions: in dim light you still can quickly detect an object with your peripheral vision, and you notice it even faster when the object wiggles. Our ancestors did not need details to identify the type of danger instantly. To see color, shape, and details, they could wait until ample light was available and use their central vision to study a relatively still object.

Sour Science
Do Sour Taste Preferences Change with Age?

DO OUR TASTES CHANGE AS WE AGE? TRY THIS PUCKER-INDUCING EXPERIMENT TO FIND OUT!

PROJECT TIME
30 minutes

KEY CONCEPTS
Biology
Taste
Food preferences
Age

Have you ever wondered if people of all ages love sour foods, or if age correlates with this preference? There are a lot of different kinds of sour candies and drinks you may have seen advertised before, some having only a mild sour flavor and others that are truly mouth puckering! In this activity, you will investigate if there is a difference between the sour preferences of kids and adults. If you developed a super-sour food, to whom would you try to sell it?

BACKGROUND

Do you know anyone who likes to eat lemons? Or loves really sour candies? Maybe you are one of those people? People have different definitions of what they find palatable, or tasty to eat. There are many different factors that go into deciding whether or not something is palatable. One of the biggest parts of that decision is how something tastes. Humans can sense five tastes: sour, salty, bitter, sweet, and umami (oo-MAH-mee), which is the non-salty part of how soy sauce tastes.

Taste is detected by the taste buds that line the tongue and other parts of the mouth. Although there is some variation from person to person, the human tongue has an average of about 10,000 taste buds. Inside each taste bud are several receptor cells. These cells can sense the five different tastes and send that information to the brain.

In addition to taste, people think about several other factors when deciding if something is acceptable to eat. These include other components of flavor, such as how spicy a food is or how it smells, the texture and temperature of a food, and whether the food is something they like eating for cultural or personal reasons.

MATERIALS

- Five containers (must be able to hold 1 quart [1 l] each)
- Citric acid, which is used for sprouting or canning foods. It can be found as a powder or granules in some grocery stores in the spices, baking supplies, or health supplements aisles. It can also be ordered online from some vitamin companies, such as LuckyVitamin.com. Caution: Only use food-grade citric acid.
- Water
- Measuring spoons
- Measuring cups
- Masking tape
- Permanent marker
- Citrus-flavored powdered drink mix, such as lemonade flavor (enough to make 4 quarts, or about 4 liters)
- 50 small paper cups
- Large work surface
- Adult volunteers (at least 5)
- Kid volunteers between the ages of 5 and 11 years old (at least 5)

PREPARATION

- Make sure the citric acid you have is food-grade citric acid.

- Into one of your containers, put 6 tablespoons of citric acid and 3 cups (710 ml) of water. Mix the citric acid mixture until all of the citric acid is dissolved.

- Each of the remaining four containers will hold a different lemonade batch. Using masking tape and a permanent marker, label each of the four containers as "1," "2," "3," or "4."

- Following the directions on the package of the lemonade drink mix, add enough of the drink mix powder to each labeled container to make 1 quart (1 l) of the drink (per container).

- In the container labeled "1," add 4 cups (946 ml) of water.

- In the container labeled "2," add 4 cups (946 ml) of water and 3 tablespoons (44 ml) of the citric acid mixture. This is similar to 10 percent lemon juice in sourness.

- In the container labeled "3," add 3 1/3 cups (787 ml) of water and 2/3 cup (157 ml) of the citric acid mixture. This is similar to 50 percent lemon juice in sourness.

- In the container labeled "4," add 2 cups (473 ml) of water and 2 cups and 2 tablespoons (503 ml) of the citric acid mixture.

- Mix each lemonade batch until the drink mix is completely dissolved. Refrigerate the containers until you are ready to have your volunteers taste test them.

- Right before taste testing, label 10 paper cups as "#1," 10 as "#2," 10 as "#3," and 10 as "#4." If you have more than 10 volunteers total, you will need to label and use more cups.

56

PROCEDURE

- On a large work surface, set out all of the labeled paper cups. Pour the lemonade batches into the appropriately labeled cups. For example, batch 1 (the lemonade without any citric acid added to it) will go in the cups labeled "#1." Try to keep each batch grouped closely together.

- Pour plain water into 10 more cups (or more if you have more than 10 volunteers total). These cups don't have to be labeled.

- Give each volunteer one cup with lemonade batch 1 and ask them to try it. Then give each volunteer a cup of water and have them take a sip to clear their palettes. *How do the volunteers react to drinking the lemonade?*

- Continue passing out the lemonade, one cup and batch at a time, asking the volunteers to taste it, and always having the volunteers take a sip of water in between tastings. *How do the volunteers react to drinking the different lemonade batches?*

- Once the volunteers have tasted all four batches of lemonade, ask them which was their favorite and which was their least favorite.

- *Do adults and kids choose different lemonades as their favorite? Did more volunteers in one age group choose the sourest lemonade as their favorite? What about as their least favorite?*

EXTRA

Try this activity again but use more volunteers, such as 15 adults and 15 kids. *When using more volunteers, do you see a stronger taste preference trend?*

⚛ SCIENCE FAIR IDEA ～～～

In this activity you investigated preferences for the taste sour. *But what kinds of preferences do people have for the other tastes (sweet, salty, bitter, and umami)? Think of a way to test these other tastes and then try it out. Do kids and adults have different preferences for other tastes?*

ExTRA ～～～

Does being a "picky" eater change how likely a person is to enjoy really sour foods? Find volunteers and ask if they're picky, normal, or adventurous eaters. Try to get at least 10 people in each category. Then repeat this activity with them. Do you see any correlations between the kind of eater a person is and whether they enjoy very sour tastes?

OBSERVATIONS AND RESULTS ··········

Did the kid volunteers like sourer lemonade batches most, whereas the adult volunteers did not? Did the adult volunteers prefer less sour lemonade batches?

One job food scientists can have is working at companies to help design new foods. One of the things they have to do is conduct sensory analysis, which is the scientific process of determining how people react to different foods, and then make decisions about whether or not they like them. Food scientists already know a lot about people's food preferences. For example, they know that babies usually prefer sweet foods, like applesauce and sweet potatoes, over more bitter foods, like broccoli. They also know that Americans and Europeans like mint-flavored toothpastes, while people in China and Japan prefer their toothpastes to be fruit-flavored. But what about sour flavors? There are a lot of sour candies and drinks advertised on TV, in magazines and in other places that tempt kids, but not many of those advertisements make the foods sound appealing to adults. There as a good reason for this: in general, kids really do prefer sour tastes much more than adults do. In a study similar to this activity, researchers found that over one-third of kids tested preferred the sourest food tested, whereas virtually none of the adults preferred this food.

CLEANUP ·····················

Pour any leftover liquid down the drain and return all materials to where you got them.

THE SCIENTIFIC METHOD

The scientific method helps scientists—and students—gather facts to prove whether an idea is true. Using this method, scientists come up with ideas and then test those ideas by observing facts and drawing conclusions. You can use the scientific method to develop and test your own ideas!

Question: What do you want to learn? What problem needs to be solved? Be as specific aspossible.

Research: Learn more about your topic and refine your question.

Hypothesis: Form an educated guess about what you think will answer your question. This allows you to make a prediction you can test.

Experiment: Create a test to learn if your hypothesis is correct. Limit the number of variables,or elements of the experiment that could change.

Analysis: Record your observations about the progress and results of your experiment. Then analyze your data to understand what it means.

Conclusion: Review all your data. Did the results of the experiment match the prediction? If so, your hypothesis was correct. If not, your hypothesis may need to be changed.

GLOSSARY

accommodate: To provide space for something.

ample: Enough or more than enough.

bind: To fasten something together.

circumference: The distance around something.

complementary: Things that go together to support each other.

convey: To communicate or pass on.

correlate: When one thing depends on another.

densely: Closely, without space between.

impending: Something that is about to happen.

palatable: Pleasant to taste.

parallel: Side by side with the same distance between.

stable: Secure, not likely to change.

stimulus: A thing or event that causes a reaction.

sustain: To bear the weight of something.

traverse: To cross through.

ADDITIONAL RESOURCES

Books

Bozzone, Donna. *The Fascinating Human Body Book for Kids: 500 Phenomenal Facts!* Emeryville, CA: Rockridge Press, 2021.

Smithsonian Institution. *Knowledge Encyclopedia Human Body!* New York, NY: DK Publishing, 2017.

Wagner, Kristie. *Human Anatomy for Kids: A Junior Scientist's Guide to How We Move, Breathe, and Grow.* Emeryville, CA: Rockridge Press, 2021.

Websites

Discovery Education
Sciencefaircentral.com

Exploratorium
www.exploratorium.edu/search/science%20fair%20projects

Science Buddies
www.sciencebuddies.org/science-fair-projects/project-ideas/list

Science Fun for Everyone!
www.sciencefun.org/?s+science+fair

Videos

Body Waste- Science Trek
https://ny.pbslearningmedia.org/resource/idptv11.sci.life.reg.d4kbw1/body-waste/

Meet My Muscles- Upper Body
https://ny.pbslearningmedia.org/resource/980ff42e-930b-4afa-b184-20f3a3c33488/meet-my-muscles-upper-body/

Meet My Muscles- Lower Body
https://ny.pbslearningmedia.org/resource/83c4de84-1589-40bc-9571-e7a65e15147f/meet-my-muscles-lower-body/

INDEX